MW01070578

★ Voices from the Civil War ★

CONFEDERATE SOLDIERS

edited by John Dunn

BLACKBIRCH®
PRESS

THOMSON

™

GALE

San Diego • Detroit • New York • San Francisco • Cleveland
New Haven, Conn. • Waterville, Maine • London • Munich

© 2003 by Blackbirch Press™. Blackbirch Press™ is an imprint of The Gale Group, Inc.,
a division of Thomson Learning, Inc.

Blackbirch Press™ and Thomson Learning™ are trademarks used herein under license.

For more information, contact
The Gale Group, Inc.
27500 Drake Rd.
Farmington Hills, MI 48331-3535
Or you can visit our Internet site at http://www.gale.com

ALL RIGHTS RESERVED
No part of this work covered by the copyright hereon may be reproduced or used in any
form or by any means—graphic, electronic, or mechanical, including photocopying, recording,
taping, Web distribution, or information storage retrieval systems—without the written
permission of the publisher.

Every effort has been made to trace the owners of copyrighted material.

Photo credits: Cover, pages 15, 17, 19, 21, 27 © CORBIS; pages 8 (Davis), 9 (Lincoln) © Digital
Stock; pages 7, 8, 9, 29 © Library of Congress; pages 5, 11, 23 © North Wind Picture Archives

LIBRARY OF CONGRESS CATALOGING-IN-PUBLICATION DATA

Dunn, John M., 1949-
   Confederate soldiers / by John M. Dunn.
     p. cm. — (Voices of the Civil War)
Summary: Provides excerpts from letters, books, newspaper articles, speeches, and
diaries which express various thoughts about the plight of southern soldiers during the
Civil War.
Includes bibliographical references and index.
  ISBN 1-56711-792-9 (hardback : alk. paper)
 1. United States—History—Civil War, 1861-1865—Personal narratives,
Confederate—Juvenile literature. 2. United States—History—Civil War, 1861-1865—
Social aspects—Juvenile literature. 3. Soldiers—Confederate States of America—Social
conditions—Sources—Juvenile literature. 4. Soldiers—Confederate States of America—
Biography—Juvenile literature. 5. Confederate States of America. Army—Biography—
Juvenile literature. [1. United States—History—Civil War, 1861-1865—Personal
narratives. 2. United States—History—Civil War, 1861-1865—Sources. 3. Soldiers—Social
conditions—19th century. 4. Confederate States of America. Army—History—Sources.] I.
Title. II. Series: Voices of the Civil War
(San Diego, Calif.)

E484.D86 2003
973.7'82—dc21
                             2002152788

Contents

DEFENDING A WAY OF LIFE

I n the summer of 1861, hundreds of thousands of boys and men across America's South answered the call of battle and went to war. Unlike any other of the nation's military conflicts, the American Civil War forced Southern men to choose between fighting for the U.S. government or for the people of their own state. For many, this was a difficult decision. For others, the choice was obvious. For decades, Southerners and Northerners had had disagreements over slavery, taxes on imports, states' rights, and other issues. Many white Southerners believed the South was so different from the rest of the United States that it deserved to be a separate country. More than a million men decided the Southern way of life was worth defending and joined the Southern military forces.

Slavery was the most troublesome issue to divide the nation. The majority of Southern men who took up arms, though, did not view themselves as fighting to uphold slavery. In fact, the average white Southerner could not afford to own slaves. Most slaves worked on large plantations run by wealthy families. On the other hand, many Southerners believed slavery added to the region's agricultural economy. Nearly all white Southerners resented being judged by Northerners over the issue. In fact, Northern criticism unified white Southerners and strengthened their resistance.

Southern males were quick to enlist when war came in 1861. Military duty had always been a strong tradition in the South. The region also had a great number of military academies. In addition, Southerners made up the majority of cadets (students) at West Point, the U.S. government's famed military academy. State militias were also trained and well manned throughout the South. Southern officers who were in the U.S. Army when war came quickly gave up their commissions to support the South's newly formed government—the Confederate States of America.

Most slaves, such as those pictured here picking and baling cotton, worked on large plantations owned by wealthy families.

Southerners from different social classes enlisted. Planters, poor farmers, laborers, middle class merchants, and lawyers became soldiers. Some Native Americans also signed up. Tribes who lived in the South, including the Cherokee, Choctaw, Chickasaw, and Seminole, formed brigades that took part in the fighting. Toward the end of the Civil War, some black slaves even fought on behalf of the South. Many were forced to fight. Others felt loyal to their masters and wanted to be at their sides in combat.

For many Southerners who enlisted, the war represented, at first, a chance to take part in a grand adventure. Thousands of young men who had never been more than fifty miles away from where they were born looked forward to the opportunity to travel to distant places.

Many Confederate volunteers traveled directly to Richmond, Virginia, the Confederate capital. Some moved to the nearest military headquarters to be trained for combat. Others gathered in town squares. They elected their own officers, usually from a handful of wealthy or important men of the town. Local girls and women sewed uniforms and flags for them. These hastily formed companies traveled by ferry, steamboat, or train to other towns within their state to merge with other military companies and form regiments. Some men walked the dusty backroads to reach their destination. Many upper class plantation owners, who were skilled horsemen, formed cavalry units and made the journey by horseback.

Though some Southerners had never fired a gun in their lives, many more had. Their numbers included men who hunted, camped, and rode horses. These skills

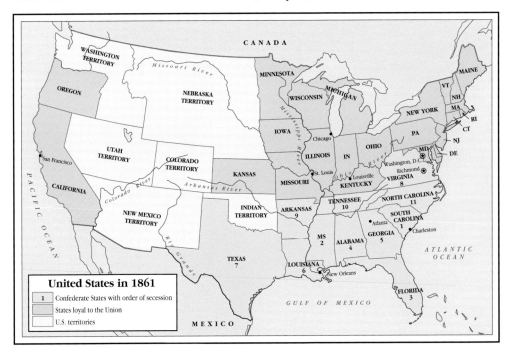

gave the Confederate armies an edge over their Union counterparts.

Discipline was often difficult to maintain among the new recruits. Southern men tended to be fiercely independent, and they did not like to obey orders. Confederate officers quickly learned that to earn their men's respect and loyalty, they had to demonstrate bravery and courage on the battlefield.

Rebel soldiers, like their Northern rivals, discovered that army camp life was miserable. Food was of poor quality, and it often spoiled and became inedible. Men were tormented by lice and other insects. Diseases such as dysentery, diphtheria, and typhoid took the lives of many men before they ever saw battle.

These hardships paled in comparison with the horrors of war, though Southern

Slain Confederate soldiers lie heaped in a ditch on a battlefield.

soldiers soon realized that war was horrible. Though conditions were terrible, Southerners rose up and met the challenges of war. Against a better equipped and numerically superior enemy, Confederate soldiers fought fiercely in battles that primarily took place on Southern soil. Many saw themselves as the defenders of their homeland against Yankee invaders. This belief kept their morale high and gave them a strong will to fight. Time and again, greatly outnumbered Southern soldiers stunned their opponents with their determination and fighting abilities. As the war dragged on, though, many rebels grew weary of the killing and wished to return home. Some had also changed their minds about why they were fighting. They started to blame the rich, slave-owning planters for causing the war.

Though Confederate soldiers often won battles, the North's superior resources eventually took a toll on the South. In the last years of fighting, many Confederate soldiers wore rags. They were dirty, barefoot, hungry, and weary of war. Victories were few and far between in 1864 and 1865. When the last of the Confederate troops surrendered in May 1865, about 258,000 Southern men were dead.

Unlike most Northerners, Southern veterans returned to their home states after the war, to find their towns, homes, and farms in ruins from neglect and the ravages of war. Both whites and blacks became homeless. Confederate money was worthless. Factories and railroads were destroyed. Northern troops occupied much of the South during the postwar years. They imposed military law upon a civilian population. Never before or since have so many American soldiers experienced the pain of military defeat on their own soil, as did the Southern fighting men.

★ Chronology of the Civil War ★

November 1860

Abraham Lincoln is elected president of the United States.

December 1860–March 1861

• Concerned about Lincoln's policy against slavery in the West, the South Carolina legislature unanimously votes to secede from the United States. Alabama, Florida, Georgia, Louisiana, Mississippi, and Texas secede from the Union, and form the Confederate States of America.

• Mississippi senator Jefferson Davis becomes president of the Confederacy.

• Arkansas, North Carolina, Tennessee, and Virginia later join the rebellion.

April 1861

Confederate troops fire on Union-occupied Fort Sumter in South Carolina and force a surrender. This hostile act begins the Civil War.

September 1862–January 1863

• Lee's Army of Northern Virginia and George McClellan's Army of the Potomac fight the war's bloodiest one-day battle at Antietam, Maryland. Though the battle is a draw, Lee's forces retreat to Virginia.

• Abraham Lincoln issues the Emancipation Proclamation that declares all slaves in Confederate states to be forever free. Three months later it takes effect.

September 1864

Atlanta, Georgia, surrenders to Union general William T. Sherman, who orders Atlanta evacuated and then burned. Over the coming months, he begins his March to the Sea to Savannah. His troops destroy an estimated $100 million worth of civilian property in an attempt to cut rebel supply lines and reduce morale.

Jefferson Davis, president of the Confederate States of America

July 1861

Confederate troops defeat Union forces at the First Battle of Manassas (First Bull Run) in Fairfax County, Virginia, the first large-scale battle of the war.

April 1862

• Confederate troops are defeated at the Battle of Shiloh in Tennessee. An estimated 23,750 soldiers are killed, wounded, or missing, more than in all previous American wars combined.

• Slavery is officially abolished in the District of Columbia; the only Union slave states left are Delaware, Kentucky, Maryland, and Missouri.

June 1862

General Robert E. Lee assumes command of the Conferate Army of Northern Virginia.

Robert E. Lee

August 1862

Confederate troops defeat Union forces at the Second Battle of Manassas (Second Bull Run) in Prince William County, Virginia.

July 1863

Union forces stop the South's invasion of the North at Gettysburg, Pennsylvania. Lasting three days, it is the bloodiest battle of the war.

November 1863

President Abraham Lincoln delivers the Gettysburg Address in honor of those who died at the war's bloodiest battle at Gettysburg.

April 1865

• Confederate general Robert E. Lee surrenders to Union general Ulysses S. Grant. This ends the Civil War on April 9.

• Five days later, President Lincoln is assassinated by actor John Wilkes Booth.

December 1865

The Thirteenth Amendment becomes law and abolishes slavery in the United States.

Abraham Lincoln, president of the United States of America

★ *Nicholas A. Davis* ★

ROAD TO RICHMOND

Texas, like the other Confederate states, responded quickly to the Confederacy's call for soldiers. Hundreds of volunteers arrived at various Camps of Instruction created by the Texas state legislature in April 1861. The purpose of these camps was to train recruits and volunteers to be soldiers. At first, the Texas state government expected that the men would fight as state troops. Confederacy officials, however, insisted that the soldiers fight under the command of the Confederacy. Finally, the men completed basic training and began a long journey to Richmond, Virginia. They were placed where the Confederate army needed them. One of these Texas soldiers was Nicholas A. Davis, a Presbyterian, who served as a chaplain (a religious leader) in General John Hood's Texas Brigade. In the following passage, Davis describes the early trips to Richmond.

GLOSSARY

- **countenances:** faces
- **animation:** vitality, spirit
- **interchanged:** exchanged, traded
- **tocsin:** alarm
- **avocations:** jobs or hobbies
- **endowed:** furnished, equipped
- **adorn:** decorate
- **communion:** fellowship
- **shrines:** altars, sanctuaries
- **sequestered:** secreted, concealed
- **scabbard:** sheath for a sword
- **venture:** risk
- **assert:** say
- **impetuous:** hasty, rash
- **enterprise:** readiness to take action
- **Southrons:** Southerners
- **adjoining:** neighboring
- **savannahs:** fields
- **imbued:** inspired
- **actuated:** motivated

• Richard B. Harwell, ed., *The Confederate Reader.* Konecky & Konecky, 1958.

The hour of departure was hailed with rejoicing by the men, and all countenances were beaming with animation; all hearts were high with hope and confidence, and every bosom seemed warmed by enthusiasm—the last greetings among friends were interchanged, the last good-byes were said, and away we sped over the flowery prairies, with colors fluttering in the breeze, each hoarse whistle of the locomotive placing distance between us and our loves at home. . . .

The men of whom we are now writing had come together from the hills and valleys of Texas, at the first sound of the tocsin of war. The first harsh blast of the bugle found them at their home, in the quiet employment of the arts and avocations of peace. It is a singular fact, but no less singular than true, that those men who, at home, were distinguished among their fellows as peculiarly endowed to adorn and enrich society by their lives and conversation, who were first in the paths of social communion, whose places when they left were unfilled, and until they return again must be deserted shrines, should be the first to leap from their sequestered seats, the first to flash the rusty steel from its scabbard, and to flash it in the first shock of battle. But so it is, and we ven-

This woodcut depicts Confederate soldiers learning knife-throwing skills in training camp. After basic training, they were sent wherever needed.

ture to assert, that of all those whom this war has drawn to the field, and torn away from the domestic fireside, there will be none so much missed at home as those who left with the first troops for Virginia. They were representative men from all portions of the State—young, impetuous and fresh, full of energy, enterprise, and fire—men of action—men who, when they first heard the shrill shriek of battle, as it came from the far-off coast of South Carolina, at once ceased to argue with themselves, or with their neighbors, as to the why-fores or the where-fores—it was enough to know that the struggle had commenced, and that they were Southrons.

Where companies had not been formed in their own counties, they hastened to adjoining counties, and there joined in with strangers. Some came in from the far-off frontier. Some came down from the hills of the North, and some came up from the savannahs of the South—all imbued with one self-same purpose, to fight for "Dixie."

Among them could be found men of all trades and professions—attorneys, doctors, merchants, farmers, mechanics, editors, scholastics, &c., &c.—all animated and actuated by the self-same spirit of patriotism, and all for the time being willing to lay aside their plans of personal ambition, and to place themselves on the altar of their country, and to put themselves under the leveling discipline of the army.

⋆ *Loreta Janeta Velazquez* ⋆

A WOMAN IN THE RANKS

*Southern and Northern women volunteered to perform a variety of noncombat
tasks during the Civil War. Some women did this to be near their brothers, husbands,
or friends. Patriotism and excitement motivated others. Women participated in the war
in many ways. Most served at army camps as nurses, water-bearers, flag-carriers, and
laundresses. Some even wore military uniforms and drilled with combat units. A few
women even disguised themselves as men and fought on the battlefields. One of them was
Loreta Janeta Velazquez. She was born in Cuba and raised in New Orleans. Posing as a
male lieutenant named Harry T. Buford, she fought for the South in a few battles and
later served as a Confederate detective and spy. The following is an excerpt from her
wartime memoirs. Velazquez recalls her thoughts as she awaited combat the night before
and the morning of the Battle of First Bull Run at Manassas, Virginia, on July 21, 1861.*

• **Richard Hall, *Patriots In Disguise: Women Warriors of the Civil War.*
  New York: Paragon House, 1993.**

I had fancied that sleep would be impossible to me under such circumstances; but
a very little experience as a soldier was sufficient for me to be able to fall into a
soldier's way of doing things, and I soon learned to take my rest as naturally and
composedly upon the bare ground as if on the most downy couch, and not even the
excitements and anxieties incident to an impending battle could prevent
my tired eyes from closing after a long and fatiguing day passed under a
broiling July sun. . . .

The [next] morning was a beautiful one, although it gave the
promise of a sweltering day; and the scene presented to my eyes, as
I surveyed the field, was one of marvelous beauty and grandeur. I
cannot pretend to express in words what I felt, as I found myself
one among thousands of combatants, who were about to engage
in a deadly and desperate struggle.

The supreme moment of my life had arrived, and all the glorious
aspirations of my romantic girlhood were on the point of realization.
I was elated beyond measure, although cool-headed enough. . . . Fear
was a word I did not know the meaning of; and as I noted the ashy
faces, and the trembling limbs of some of the men about me, I
almost wished that I could feel a little fear, if only for the sake of
sympathizing with the poor devils. I do not say this for brag, for
I despise braggarts as much as I do cowards.

🖋 GLOSSARY

- **fancied:** imagined
- **composedly:** freed
  from worry
- **downy:** feathery
- **anxieties:** worries
- **incident:** related
- **impending:**
  approaching
- **fatiguing:**
  exhausting
- **sweltering:** hot
  and humid
- **surveyed:** observed
- **aspirations:**
  desires
- **elated:** thrilled

★ *An Unknown Soldier* ★

RETREAT FROM SHILOH

One of the deadliest battles of the Civil War took place in 1862 at Shiloh, Tennessee. At nearby Pittsburg Landing, forty-two thousand Union troops led by General Ulysses S. Grant waited for reinforcements who were advancing from the northeast. Once united, the two Union forces planned to invade Mississippi, a Confederate state. Meanwhile, twenty-two miles to the southwest at Corinth, Mississippi, forty-one thousand Confederate soldiers under General Albert Sidney Johnston readied for a fight. Aware of the danger of an invasion, Johnston ordered his men to attack Grant's men at Pittsburg Landing before the Union reinforcements could arrive. Heavy fighting began April 6. Three days later, a total of twenty-four thousand men from both sides were dead or wounded. More men died at Shiloh than had fallen during all previous American wars combined. Though they suffered great losses from Johnston's attack, Grant's forces rallied when the Union reinforcements finally arrived and turned the Southerners away. The following account by an unknown rebel soldier on horseback describes the panic and terror that struck the Confederates as they retreated from the battlefield.

- **Harold Elk Straubing, ed., *Civil War Eyewitness Reports*. Hamden, CT: Archon Books, 1985.**

I n this ride I saw more of human agony and woe than I trust I shall ever again be called to behold. The retreating host wound along a narrow and almost impossible road. Here was a long line of wagons loaded with wounded piled in like bags of grain, groaning and cursing; while the mules plunged on in mud and water, the latter sometimes coming into the wagons. Next was a struggling regiment of infantry, pressing on past the train of wagons; then a stretcher, borne upon the shoulders of four men, carrying a wounded officer; then soldiers staggering along, with an arm broken and hanging down or other fearful wounds. To add to the horrors of the scene, the elements of heaven marshaled their forces—a fitting accompaniment of the tempest of human desolation and passion which was raging. A cold drizzling rain commenced about nightfall, and finally turned to pitiless, blinding hail. I passed wagon trains filled with wounded and dying soldiers, without even a blanket to shield them from the driving sleet and hail which fell in stones as large as partridge eggs, until it lay on the ground two inches deep. Some three hundred men died during that awful retreat, and their bodies were thrown out to make room for others who, although wounded, had struggled on through the storm hoping to find shelter, rest, and medical care.

> **GLOSSARY**
> - **host:** crowd
> - **borne:** carried
> - **marshaled their forces:** came together and rained
> - **tempest:** storm
> - **desolation:** gloom
> - **commenced:** began

★ *Randolph A. Shotwell* ★
SHOCK OF LIFE IN AN ARMY CAMP

The grim reality of army camp life came as a shock to many young men who volunteered to fight in the Civil War. Living conditions were usually cramped and dirty. Many new soldiers also had difficulty accepting the authority of officers who tried to instill military discipline in their men. Others had trouble getting along with fellow soldiers who came from different social, economic, or educational backgrounds. In addition, some soldiers missed pleasures such as books and intelligent conversation. Randolph A. Shotwell, a private in the Eighth Virginia Infantry, learned what army camp was like in August 1861. At the age of sixteen, he ran away from a college preparatory school in Pennsylvania. He then made his way to the front lines, and joined the first Confederate regiment he came across. In the following excerpt, Shotwell describes his impressions of his first day in a Confederate camp.

GLOSSARY
- **vacant:** empty
- **exclamations:** cries
- **bade:** told
- **prone:** lying flat
- **sultry:** humid
- **precursor:** sign
- **disproportion:** inequality
- **calamitous:** disastrous
- **temperament:** mood, attitude
- **rollicking:** playful
- **predilections:** inclinations
- **consumptive:** related to tuberculosis, a wasting disease of the lungs
- **deprivations:** losses
- **ineradicable:** permanent, incapable of being rid of
- **vermin:** insects and other pests
- **mortification:** humiliation
- **domineer:** command

- **Randolph Abbott Shotwell, *The Papers of Randolph Abbott Shotwell*, vol. I, ed. by J.G. de Roulhac Hamilton. Raleigh: North Carolina Historical Commission, 1929**

The captain peered into tent after tent seeking a vacant corner to "stow away" the new recruit, but at each was greeted by a chorus of exclamations that there was not an inch of room: that the occupants were already "thick as fleas"! At length, at the last tent, the very bottom of the row in more than one respect, he bade me enter. "Crowd up, men, crowd up!"—he cried—"make room for this new man." There were seven large men rustling amid the straw and swearing they were already packed one on top of another. "Can't help it"—said he—"you must squeeze in somehow." This last remark was addressed to me. Then he walked off to have a smoke with the colonel, leaving me to find a bed if I could.

It was too dark to distinguish faces, but the spectacle of seven men prone in the straw was so much like a pig-pen that I laughed outright, whereupon one of them recognized me, and amid much cursing of the officers made room for me "spoon-fashion." However, I soon crawled out to sit in the doorway. The night was very hot and sultry—precursor of a thunder-storm, and the odor of seven pairs of unwashed feet filled the interior of the tent with nauseating oppressiveness.

Confederate soldiers pose in camp in 1861. The harshness of army camp life was a difficult adjustment for most recruits.

Right here let me suggest that perhaps few readers appreciate the difference,—the disproportion, in the sacrifices of different persons, and classes in our calamitous struggle for Southern freedom. Differences in health, in wealth, in temperament, in culture, in social relations, and in domestic circumstances were so great that there could be no sort of comparison between the patriotism of different members of the same company, from the same country, or even family.

Take, for example, a wild rollicking youngster, without family ties, fond of outdoor life, and male companionship, careless of books or newspapers, and easily amused by a game of cards, "a fight or a footrace," who would therefore rather volunteer than to stay at home and work in the shop or on the farm. What equality of sacrifice was there in his case as compared with another young man of the same age, with a wife and children needing his care, or an aged mother, begging him to stay; with no predilections for a hardy life, but with a thousand reasons for pursuing other plans, yet who drops all personal considerations, leaves his family to the charity of outsiders, and goes forth to obey the call of his State! Or how shall we adjust the difference between the strong healthy man who, after marching all day, slept like a log, while his weakly comrade staggered wearily into camp three hours behind the rest and sat all night propped against a tree, barking with a consumptive cough! Both may have been patriotic, but surely not equal in self-sacrifice.

Camp-life to one may not always have been *pleasant*; but to the other it was *continual misery*. Some men suffered from *deprivations*, such as books, letters, and intellectual food, which were never once thought of by the majority of their comrades.

Some men were accustomed to rough ways of living before they volunteered in the army; whereas, for my part I can truthfully say I suffered more from coarse dirty food, dirty blankets and clothes; unwashed linen, (often marching and fighting for weeks without opportunity to wash our faces once a day,) and the ineradicable camp-vermin, than from all other hardships of the service. Perhaps I ought to include the bitter mortification of having to obey in silence the coarse commands of petty upstarts from corporals to captains and colonels, vulgar in speech manner, and action, but clothed with "a little brief authority" which gave them opportunity to domineer over men in every respect their superiors.

★ *Willie Barrow* ★
A PRISONER OF WAR

Tens of thousands of soldiers on both sides were taken as prisoners during the Civil War. Most were transported to various camps that were scattered across the United States. Some of the prisoners were treated well. Other prisoners lived in cramped, overcrowded, filthy, disease-ridden conditions. They endured extreme hardships and miseries for months and even years of captivity. Prison officials in many of the camps seldom had enough food, medical supplies, or even clothing for the inmates. As a result, thousands died from disease, exposure, and starvation. Sometimes, prisoners of war were forced to travel great distances to reach the prison camps. Confederate soldier Willie Barrow, from St. Francisville, Louisiana, survived the bloody Battle of Shiloh, Tennessee, in April 1862, only to become a prisoner of war. In the following diary entries, Barrow tells of the two-week journey he endured while being transported by river to a Union prison camp in Chicago, Illinois.

- **"Civil War Diary of William Micajah Barrow,"** *Louisiana Historical Quarterly*, **October 1934.**

Wednesday, 9th. This morning I awoke early after setting up half the night with the wounded. They were all much better. They began moving them about nine o'clock to the river; about one I went with one load. Got to the river at two o'clock and a man separated me from the wounded and carried me to [Union] General Buell's quarters on the Empress [a steamboat]. He had me sent to the provost-marshal and from there I went where the rest of the prisoners were.

Thursday, 10th. This morning I was up early as there was no use to attempt to sleep. We had nothing to eat until nine o'clock when they brought us a barrel of crackers and some bacon. We fried the bacon on sticks. Lord deliver me from such hardships. Sitting on the ground trying to keep warm our eyes filled with smoke and no handkerchief to blow my nose on. Sky cloudy.

Friday, April 11th. This morning it commenced to rain. We had nothing to eat but what was given to us the day before. We [stayed] in the rain trying to keep as dry as possible before the fires. About two o'clock the provost-marshal came and called us out in two ranks and called the roll to see if we were all there; they then marched us between two rows of Wisconsin troops to the river where we got aboard the Woodford [another ship]. I slept on some straw; went to bed without anything to eat, but slept pretty sound notwithstanding the poor accommodations. . . .

GLOSSARY

- **quarters:** lodgings
- **provost-marshal:** an officer who is in charge of the military police
- **commenced:** began
- **accommodations:** room and board
- **dysentery:** severe diarrhea caused by infection

This photo of a prison camp for Confederate soldiers shows the crowded, dirty conditions typical of such camps.

Sunday, April 13th. This morning I awoke bright and early as usual. Had for breakfast a hard cracker and some coffee. Got a little soap and succeeded in getting a little dirt off my hands. For dinner I had the same as for breakfast, a hard biscuit and some coffee. We were in the Mississippi river running five miles an hour. Weather cool but pleasant I changed my bed from the straw to some hard boards. Monday, April 14th. This morning I awoke and found myself in St. Louis, Mo.

April 23rd. We [stayed] in St. Louis for two or three days and from there came to Chicago, Camp Douglas, where they keep all their prisoners. The reason I have not kept up my regular journal is that I have been suffering from [dysentery]. The weather here is very cold and goes very hard with the boys from the south.

★ *John Dooley* ★

THE BATTLE OF SECOND BULL RUN

In the summer of 1862, Confederate forces under General Robert E. Lee clashed with Union troops at the Second Battle of Bull Run at Manassas, Virginia. At this site more than a year before, the two sides had met in the first great land battle of the war. That First Battle of Bull Run had ended in a Southern victory. Though this second contest was also won by the Confederates, many lives were lost. Added together, twenty-five thousand Union and Confederate men were killed, wounded, or missing. Confederate private John Dooley witnessed the Second Battle of Bull Run. His account of a failed Northern charge shows the tragic and bloody nature of the Civil War.

- **Joseph T. Durkin, ed., *John Dooley, Confederate Soldier*. Washington, DC: Georgetown Univ. Press, 1945.**

Yes! Here they come! Four or five lines of fresh troops deploy in the open plain in our front and direct their charge directly against that copse of woods off to our right. Oh, this is a splendid sight and one which the disinterested might well go in raptures over. Line after line of the best of the Yankee army steadily advances—and as orderly as if on parade; and it seems as tho' there was a slight cessation in the frightful roar of the artillery and musketry as these well drilled troops press on over the blood red plain.

At every step they take they see the piles of wounded and slain and their feet are slipping in the blood and brains of their comrades. Shells burst among them and a desultory musketry fire helps to thin their ranks; but still on they press. . . . Many of their officers may be plainly distinguished riding beside their Brigades and Divisions, while the Stars and Stripes boastfully flaunt out defiance in the advance of each [Regiment].

On they come over dead and dying right at the copse of woods. The order is given, "Charge!", and at a double quick the foremost lines charge against the woods. They are scarcely 50 or 80 [yards] distant when a volume of smoke almost obscures the woods from our sight and volley after volley thunders against those ill fated columns. In vain does line after line advance at a run. Torn and bleeding they are hurled back, scattered, routed in confusion over the plain (blue with their slain). In vain do their officers dash in the midst of this storm of shell and bullets. The fugitives will not be rallied, but, broken and dismayed, are pursued by our victorious troops until darkness closes around.

GLOSSARY
- **deploy:** line up
- **copse:** thicket
- **disinterested:** unconcerned
- **raptures:** joys
- **cessation:** halt
- **desultory:** irregular
- **flaunt:** wave
- **obscures:** hides
- **columns:** lines of soldiers
- **rallied:** reorganized into battle lines
- **dismayed:** shocked

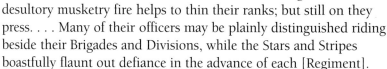

★ *John Munson* ★
SERVING IN MOSBY'S RANGERS

Colonel John Singleton Mosby was a small man who once was jailed for shooting a fellow law student. He became one of the South's best known guerrilla fighters during the Civil War. As a guerrilla, Mosby fought in an independent military unit. This group sabotaged and harassed Northern troops. Known as the "Gray Ghost" by Union troops, Mosby led his Confederate Rangers in attacks against Northern soldiers. They stole horses, robbed trains, and blew up enemy bridges and rail lines. One of the rangers who rode with Mosby's band was John Munson. He left a written account of his experiences during the war. In this excerpt, Munson describes how life in the Rangers differed from service in other army units.

A few of John S. Mosby's Rangers during the Civil War. The Rangers were a fierce band of guerrilla fighters.

• **Henry Steele Commager, ed.,** *The Blue and the Gray: The Story of the Civil War as Told by Participants.* **New York: Fairfax Press, 1960.**

The life led by Mosby's men was entirely different from that of any other body of soldiers during the war. His men had no camps nor fixed quarters, and never slept in tents. They did not even know anything about pitching a tent. The idea of making coffee, frying bacon, or soaking hardtack was never entertained. When we wanted to eat we stopped at a friendly farm house, or went into some little town and bought what we wanted. Every man in the Command had some special farm he could call his home. . . .

As a Command we had no knowledge of the first principles of cavalry drill, and could not be formed in a straight line had there been any need for our doing so. We did not know the bugle calls, and very rarely had roll-call. . . .

"Something gray" was the one requisite of our dress and the cost of it mattered little. . . . Some of the Command were extremely fastidious in the manner of dress and affected gold braid, buff trimmings, and ostrich plumes in their hats. . . . At all times, whether things went well or ill, the Guerrillas were . . . blithe in the face of danger, full of song and story, indifferent to the events of tomorrow, and keyed up to a high pitch of anticipation.

GLOSSARY
- **quarters:** lodgings
- **hardtack:** a hard biscuit
- **entertained:** considered
- **command:** military unit
- **requisite:** requirement
- **fastidious:** fussy
- **affected:** displayed
- **blithe:** cheerful
- **indifferent:** uncaring
- **anticipation:** expectation

★ *An Unknown Soldier* ★
TORMENTED BY LICE

Among the many miseries endured by soldiers of both sides of the Civil War were body lice. These small, wingless, flattened insects bit soldiers on their scalps, sucked their blood, and laid their eggs (or nits) on shafts of hair. Lice thrived in cramped, unsanitary places such as battlefields and army camps. Also able to live temporarily on clothes and bedding, they were hard to get rid of, and soldiers often complained of being "lousy," or lice-ridden. Lice bites caused discomfort and itching and often became infected. Almost nothing prevented lice from reappearing and spreading from one soldier to the next. One unknown Confederate private noted the troubles with lice in the following excerpt, written during a military campaign in Maryland in September 1862. Soldiers who had lice were usually embarrassed in front of the other men. They often battled the pests in private.

• **Richard Wheeler,** *Voices of the Civil War.* **New York: Penguin Books, 1990.**

These insects, which in camp parlance were called "graybacks," first made their appearance in the winter of 1861. At first the soldier was mortified, and felt almost disgraced at discovering one of these insects on his person . . . and energetic efforts were made to hide the secret and eliminate the cause. At first the soldier used to steal out companionless and alone, and hide in the woods and bushes, with as much secretness and caution as if he were going to commit some fearful crime. Once hid from the eyes of men, he would pursue and murder the crawling insects with a vengeful pleasure, thinking that now he would have peace and comfort of mind. . . . On his stealthy way back he would be sure to run in on a dozen solitary individuals, who tried to look unconcerned, as if indeed they were in the habit of retiring in the dim recesses of the forest for private meditation.

The satisfaction he felt would not last long. In a day or two his body would be infested again. . . . It was simply impossible to exterminate them. . . . Once lodged in the seams of the clothing, they remained until time moldered the garments. You might scald, scour, scrub, cleanse, rub, purify, leave them in [seething] liquid, or bury the raiment in the ground; but it was wasted labor, for the insects seemed to enjoy the process, and increased and multiplied under it.

On this march, particularly, when the troops had no change of clean clothes for weeks, the soldiers were literally infested with them. Many used to place their under raiment, during the night, in the bottom of some stream, and put a large stone to keep them down. In the

GLOSSARY

- **parlance:** talk
- **mortified:** embarrassed
- **steal out:** sneak away
- **stealthy:** sneaky
- **exterminate:** kill
- **moldered:** turned to dust
- **seething:** boiling
- **raiment:** article of clothing
- **bivouacked:** temporarily camped
- **denuded:** undressed

The cramped, filthy conditions of army camp life turned many once-proud Confederate soldiers into ragged, lice-ridden beggars like these pitiful men.

morning they would hastily dry them, and get a temporary relief. Every evening in Maryland, when the army halted and bivouacked for the night, hundreds of the soldiers could be seen sitting on the roads or fields, half denuded, with their clothes in their laps, busily cracking, between the two thumb-nails, these creeping nuisances.

★ Edmund Dewitt Patterson ★

A NORTHERN-BORN CONFEDERATE DEFENDS HIS ADOPTED SOUTH

Those who fought in the Civil War often chose to defend the region of the country they loved best, even if they were born elsewhere. Such was the case of Edmund Dewitt Patterson. Born and raised in Lorain County, Ohio, Patterson moved to Alabama when he was seventeen and became attached to the Southern way of life. In April 1861, he joined the Confederate army and fought against the North for the next two and a half years. Though he survived many major battles, Patterson was captured at the Battle of Gettysburg, Pennsylvania, in July 1863. He was sent to prison on Johnson's Island—an island in Lake Erie. While there, he vowed in a personal letter that the South would never surrender, no matter how badly it suffered at the hands of the enemy.

- **Edmund Dewitt Patterson,** *Yankee Rebel: The Civil War Journal of Edmund Dewitt Patterson.* **Chapel Hill: University of North Carolina Press, 1966.**

Now, I am a prisoner of war on the little island of Lake Erie, and with a prospect before me anything but cheering; entirely separated and cut off from the outside world, unable to take any active part in the struggle which is still going on between justice and injustice, right and wrong, freedom and oppression, unable to strike a blow in the glorious cause of Southern independence.

Now, the end of the war seems more distant than ever. Time only shows on the part of the abolition government a firmer determination than ever to subjugate; while on the other hand time only shows on the part of the South a stronger determination to fight to the bitter end, trusting alone to the god of battles for success at last. And we *will* succeed. Who will say that a country such as ours, rich in everything that makes a nation great and prosperous, a country with broad valleys unequalled in fertility by any others upon which the sun shines, a country abounding in natural fortresses and inhabited by eight millions of brave people determined to be free and willing to sacrifice everything even life itself upon the altar of their country, united as no people ever were before, I ask, who will say, in view of all this, that the South will not be free. I engaged in this war firmly believing that the South would be successful and now after nearly three years of war, I find that time has only served to

GLOSSARY

- **prospect:** possibility
- **abolition:** elimination of slavery
- **subjugate:** crush
- **engaged:** took part
- **verdure:** green vegetation
- **transformed:** changed
- **edifices:** buildings
- **hirelings:** workers for hire

A ragged inmate offers to sell some bread to his fellows in this woodcut depicting life at the Civil War prison camp on Johnson's Island in Lake Erie.

strengthen that opinion. I believe that winter will pass and spring come again with its verdure and flowers—I believe it as I believe anything that I see around me, the fair fields of the South may be transformed into deserts, and the places where now may be seen stately edifices, tokens of wealth and refinement, may be made as howling wildernesses, Yankee hirelings may occupy every state, every County in the South, they may occupy our state capitols and our seaport towns,—but our hill tops and hollows,—never. We will carry on the war even there.

★ *Albert T. Goodloe* ★
COOKING WITHOUT PANS

Eating well was difficult, if not impossible, for most Civil War soldiers. In camp, soldiers received fresh meat, bread, and vegetables. Many also bought prepared food from vendors called sutlers. When soldiers were on a military campaign, however, they had to rely on field rations. These rations consisted mainly of coffee (or a coffee substitute such as chicory), hard bread, and salted meat. For Northern troops, the bread was usually flour-and-water biscuits called hardtack. Confederate soldiers, on the other hand, used grated corn to make their bread. Such meals were seldom filling or nourishing, so many soldiers foraged in the countryside for berries and game. A shortage of cooking utensils also made cooking difficult. Because pots, pans, and skillets were often lost or stolen, soldiers had to be creative. Lieutenant Albert T. Goodloe of the Thirty-fifth Alabama Infantry explains in the following excerpt how his men managed to prepare their food.

• *Voices of the Civil War.* **Alexandria, VA: Time-Life Books, 1996.**

Sometimes we were supplied with cooking utensils, and sometimes we were not. For a long time, in some of the stages of the war, we baked our bread on an old broken piece of flat iron that we had picked up among the rubbish of a town near our encampment, and cooked our meat (beef) by holding it to the fire on a stick or ramrod; and not unfrequently we were put to the necessity of baking our bread in the ashes. We usually had some kind of tin, good or indifferent, to make up the dough in, but we sometimes had to use hickory bark peeled off in large pieces for that purpose, and would right often cut out a tray in the top of a log.

Among our cooking utensils mention must be made of the frying pans that we made by bursting open Yankee canteens, which we would hold over the fire by slipping the edge of the half canteen into the split end of a stick, which served as a handle. These canteens were made of two concavo-convex tin plates, fastened together around their edges and which could easily be blown open by putting a little powder in them and igniting it. We would only thus destroy the canteen as such when it began to leak, for we needed all the canteens we could get for carrying water, and then we would use the side that did not leak for a frying pan. This utensil was especially adapted for making cush in out of our bread when it was too old to be good eating otherwise; and our cush was so palatable at times that we would declare that we were going to live on cush altogether when we got home from the war.

GLOSSARY

- **ramrod:** rod used to load shot down the barrel of a rifle
- **tin:** a can
- **Yankee:** Northerner
- **concavo-convex:** curved
- **cush:** a cornmeal pancake
- **palatable:** tasty

★ Edward P. Alexander ★

KEEPING SOUTHERN TROOPS SUPPLIED

Never before in U.S. history had so many Americans taken part in a war. Not every-one fought, however. Many men worked behind the front lines. For every soldier who experienced combat in the Civil War, many more men worked far from the fighting. Their job was to keep their fellow soldiers fed, clothed, and equipped to wage war. One of those who served in this manner was Edward P. Alexander, chief of ordnance (war supplies) for the Army of Northern Virginia. In the following excerpt, Alexander describes how he kept the Army of Northern Virginia supplied with weapons and other equipment. One of his special tasks was to provide Southern troops with rifled muskets. Unlike older guns that many soldiers used at the start of the war, these newer weapons had rifling, or grooves, cut into the inside of the barrel. This rifling gave spin to the fired musket ball that made the weapon more accurate.

- **Henry Steele Commager, *The Blue and the Gray: The Story of the Civil War as Told by Participants*. New York: Fairfax Press, 1960.**

Briefly, my duties embraced the supply of arms and ammunition to all troops in the field—infantry, artillery, and cavalry. I organized the depart-ment, with an . . . officer or sergeant in every regiment, from whom I received weekly statements showing the arms and ammunition on hand in car-tridge boxes and regimental wagons. Reserve storehouses [of arms] were provided at the nearest railroad points, and . . . trains . . . to run between the storehouses and the troops. For emergency, . . . was held a train of ammunition . . . and wagons equipped with tools and expert mechanics for all sorts of repairs. . . .

In the early stages we had great trouble with the endless variety of arms and calibres in use, scarcely ten per cent of them being the muzzle-loading rifle musket, calibre .58. . . .

The old smooth-bore musket, calibre .69, made up the bulk of the Confederate armament at the beginning, some of the guns . . . being old flint-locks. But every effort was made to replace them by rifled muskets captured in battle, brought through the blockade. . . , or manufactured at a few small arsenals which we gradually fitted up. Not until after the Battle of Gettysburg [1863] was the whole army of Virginia equipped with the rifled musket.

> **GLOSSARY**
> - **Calibres:** ammuni-tion sizes
> - **Smooth bore:** gun barrel without rifling
> - **Blockade:** the Union navy block-aded Southern ports throughout the war
> - **Arsenal:** ammuni-tion storehouse

★ *W. F. Aycock* ★
A TRAGIC LETTER

Joshua K. Callaway was a schoolteacher, husband, and father when he enlisted in the Twenty-eighth Alabama Infantry Regiment at the age of twenty-seven. Later, as a soldier in the Army of the Tennessee, he fought for the Confederacy in Mississippi, Kentucky, Tennessee, and Georgia. From April 1862 to November 1863, he faithfully wrote to his wife at least twice a week, telling the story of his life as a soldier. W.F. Aycock wrote the final letter concerning Callaway's war experiences on December 5, 1863, though. This was fifteen days after the Union army attacked Confederate strongholds in the mountains near Chattanooga, Tennessee. There, at a place called Missionary Ridge, Callaway died in battle. The following is a copy of Aycock's letter to Callaway's widow with the details of her husband's death.

- **Judith Lee Hallock, ed.,** *The Civil War Letters of Joshua K. Callaway.* **Athens: University of Georgia Press, 1997.**

 Mrs. J.K. Callaway: It now falls to my unhappy lot to write you a short letter letting you know what has become of your much beloved and devoted husband Lieut. Joshua K. Callaway who fell in the late battle on Missionary Ridge, mortally wounded while rallying his company he was shot through the bowels with a [minié] ball. We picked him up, started off the field with him when he asked us to lay him down and let him die. We laid him down. We were then compelled to leave him. I don't know that he is dead but feel satisfied that he is dead. In his death the country lost one of her bravest sons, the company to which he belonged a gallant and much beloved officer. Never can his place in the [company] be filled. I feel at a loss without him as we started out in a mess together and remained together till he was wounded. I have every reason to believe that he is gone to a better land where there is no more war. . . . left some clothing; also some bed clothing he left . . . 1 jacket 2 shirts 2 . . . also left a . . . there is nothing in the satchel though. It is locked and key gone. I want you to write to me as soon as you get this letter and let me know what disposition to make of his things his . . . clothes. I think I can send along also his . . . If it be your wish I will try and send all his things home his bedding will demand a good price here and if you are willing or rather I would I can sell them and send you the money. He has left one [month's] pay account [which] it will take to pay the debts he owes in the [regiment which] I shall

GLOSSARY

- **mortally wounded:** suffering a wound that eventually caused death
- **rallying:** reorganizing and reinspiring
- **minié ball:** rifle bullet
- **compelled:** forced
- **what disposition to make of:** what to do with

A woodcut depicts the scene at Missionary Ridge, in eastern Tennessee, where Union troops attacked rebel strongholds in 1863.

collect and pay his debts. The remainder I will forward on to you also will send you a final statement of the [balance] wages due him.

The company and officers deeply sympathize with you in his loss but what is your and our loss is his eternal gain.

W. F. Aycock
Lieut. Co. K 28th Ala. Regt.

★ *Louis Leon* ★
NO REGRETS

After Union forces conquered Richmond, Virginia, the capital of the Confederacy, on April 2, 1865, a humiliated South was soon forced to surrender. News of the Confederacy's defeat came as a bitter disappointment to many Southern soldiers. One of these was Louis Leon, a private in a North Carolina regiment, who spent the final days of the war as a prisoner. Leon recorded many of his reflections on the Civil War in a diary that he kept during his four years as a Confederate soldier. In the following excerpt, Leon expresses anger over having to swear his allegiance to the U.S. government as a condition for being set free at war's end.

- **Louis Leon, *Diary of A Tar Heel Confederate Soldier.* Charlotte, NC: Stone, 1913.**

April: I suppose the end is near, for there is no more hope for the South to gain her independence. On the 10th of this month we were told by an officer that all those who wished to get out of prison by taking the oath of allegiance to the United States could do so in a very few days. There was quite a consultation among the prisoners. On the morning of the 12th we heard that [Confederate General Robert E.] Lee had surrendered on the 9th, and about 400, myself with them, took the cursed oath and were given transportation to wherever we wanted to go. I took mine to New York City to my parents, whom I have not seen since 1858. Our cause is lost; our comrades who have given their lives for the independence of the South have died in vain; that is, the cause for which they gave their lives is lost, but they positively did not give their lives in vain. They gave it for a most righteous cause, even if the cause was lost. Those that remain to see the end for which they fought—what have we left? Our sufferings and privations would be nothing had the end been otherwise, for we have suffered hunger, been without sufficient clothing, barefooted, lousy, and have suffered more than any one can believe, except soldiers of the Southern Confederacy. And the end of all is a desolated home to go to. When I commenced this diary of my life as a Confederate soldier I was full of hope for the speedy termination of the war, and our independence. I was not quite nineteen years old. I am now twenty-three. The four years that I have given to my country I do not regret, nor am I sorry for one day that I have given—my only regret is that we have lost that for which we fought. Nor do I for one moment think

GLOSSARY

- **consultation:** conversation about what to do
- **righteous:** moral and just
- **privations:** hardships
- **lousy:** covered with lice
- **desolated:** deserted or destroyed
- **commenced:** began
- **termination:** end

This photo shows the utter destruction inflicted by Union forces in 1865 on Richmond, Virginia, the stately capital city of the Confederacy. Richmond's fall was soon followed by the South's surrender.

that we lost it by any other way than by being outnumbered at least five if not ten to one. The world was open to the enemy, but shut out to us. I shall now close this diary in sorrow, but to the last I will say that, although but a private, I still say our cause was just, nor do I regret one thing that I have done to cripple the North.

★ *Robert Stiles* ★

DEATH OF A DYING UNION SOLDIER

On the morning of May 4, 1864, Union general George Meade led 110,000 men of the Army of the Potomac toward the Rapidan River in Virginia. Sixty-thousand Confederate soldiers waited for them in the dense brush. The next day was the start of intense, bloody fighting that lasted a month. In this passage, Confederate Robert Stiles tells of his encounter with a dying Union soldier he found after a battle.

• **Richard Wheeler, *Voices of the Civil War.* New York: Penguin Books, 1990.**

When it became evident that the [Union] attack had failed, I suggested to the chaplain . . . that there might be some demand for his ministrations where the enemy had broken over; so we walked there. . . . It was almost dark, but as we drew near we saw a wounded Federal soldier clutch the pantaloons of Captain Hunter, who at that moment was passing by, frying pan in hand, and heard him ask, with intense eagerness, "Can you pray, sir? Can you pray?"

The old captain looked down at him with a peculiar expression and pulled away, saying, "No, my friend. I don't wish you any harm now, but praying's not exactly my trade."

I said to the chaplain, "Let's go to that man."

As we came up, he caught my pants in the same way and uttered the same words, "Can you pray, sir? Can you pray?"

I bent over the poor fellow, turned back his blouse, and saw that a large canister shot had passed through his chest. . . . We both knelt down by him, and I took his hand in mine and said, "My friend, you haven't much time left for prayer, but if

📖 GLOSSARY

• **evident:** clear
• **chaplain:** a military clergyman
• **ministrations:** religious assistance
• **pantaloons:** trousers
• **uttered:** said
• **canister shot:** fragment from a cannon shell

you will say after me just these simple words, with heart as well as lips, all will be well with you: 'God have mercy on me, a sinner, for Jesus Christ's sake.'"

I never saw such intensity in human gaze, nor ever heard such intensity in human voice, as in the gaze and voice of that dying man as he held my hand and looked into my face, repeating the simple, awful, yet reassuring words I had dictated. He uttered them again and again, with the death rattle in his throat and the death tremor in his frame, until someone shouted, "They are coming again!" and we broke away. . . . It proved to be a false alarm, and we returned immediately—but he was dead; yes, dead and half-stripped.

FOR FURTHER READING

Books

Harnett T. Kane, *A Picture Story of the Confederacy*. New York: Lothrop, Lee & Shepard, 1965. This illustrated book focuses on the men who fought for the Confederacy.

Earl Schenk Miers, *Billy Yank and Johnny Reb: How They Fought and Made Up*. Chicago: Rand McNally, 1959. A very readable account of the war told from the viewpoints of common soldiers on both sides and the citizens who lived through the conflict.

Douglas J. Savage, *Rangers, Jayhawkers, and Bushwhackers in the Civil War*. Philadelphia: Chelsea House, 2000. This interesting book tells the story of the 'irregular' soldiers—the guerrillas and rangers—who fought on both sides of the conflict.

Linda R. Wade, *The Men Who Fought the Civil War*. Edina, MN: Abdo, 1998. In addition to providing information about generals and soldiers, this volume also features the views of chaplains, newspapermen, and others involved in the Civil War. The roles of women in the war are also discussed.

G. Clifton Wisler, *When Johnny Went Marching: Young Americans Fight the Civil War*. New York: HarperCollins, 2001. A fascinating collection of stories of forty-nine young people—boys and girls—who took part in the Civil War as drummers, soldiers, spies, and many other occupations.

Websites

The American Civil War Home Page
http://sunsite.utk.edu/civil-war The largest online directory of Civil War resources, maintained by Dr. George H. Hoemann of the University of Tennessee. Includes biographical information on Confederate generals.

The Civil War Home Page
http://www.civil-war.net A database of Civil War history, with detailed information on specific battles and campaigns.

INDEX